Grandma's Little Activity Book

Fun Things To Do With Your Grandkids

by

Margolyn Woods

Tulsa, Oklahoma

All Scripture quotations are taken from the *King James Version* of the Bible.

Grandma's Little Activity Book
 Fun Things To Do With Your Grandkids
ISBN 1-56292-068-5
Copyright © 1994 by Margolyn Woods
Oklahoma City, Oklahoma 73131

Published by Honor Books
P.O. Box 55388
Tulsa, Oklahoma 74155

Grandma's Little Activity Book

Fun Things To Do With Your Grandkids

Grandma's Little Activity Book is dedicated to great grand-parents, Ole and Vivian Johnson, and to a special adopted grandparent, Mary Baker.

Train up a child in the way that he
should go and even when he is
old he will not depart from it.
Proverbs 22:6

Introduction

There is a special bond that exists between grandparents and their grandchildren. It goes beyond simply a family tie, but stretches into warm friendship. Memories abound of the grandpa that taught you how to fish, or the grandma that made pies just the way you liked them.

Now it's your turn to make those special memories with your grandchildren. Honor Books is proud to present to you *Grandma's Little Activity Book*. This heart-warming and fun book is filled with wonderful ideas for grandparents to do with their grandkids when they come for a visit. Written by Margolyn Woods, herself a grandmother, the activities in this book will strengthen the bond between your grandchildren and you. The friendly design and delightful illustrations inside *Grandma's Little Activity Book* make this a book that is certain to be treasured by both you and your grandkids for a lifetime.

Grandma's Little Activity Book will build relationships in the institution most vital to the future of children today — the family.

Many schools welcome volunteer grandparents. Your grandchild will cherish your involvement. You might listen as children read out loud, or help with playground duty at recess. Both you and your grandchild will greatly benefit from your participation!

Batter up!

Grandpa, build memories with your grandchildren by taking them to a professional ball game nearby. Prior to the game spend some time with your grandchildren getting familiar with the players who will be in the game. Save room for hot dogs and soda!

*Y*our day!

*A*sk your grandchild what special activity they would like to do. (If you have any limitations be sure to explain them before they start planning.) Then follow through with the plan. Your grandchild will be pleased to plan the day! (Be sure to have an idea ready if they can't come up with any.)

Rough it!

*E*very child loves a camp out! Pitch a tent in the "wild jungle" of the den, or the "deep forest" under the stairs. The tent can be an old sheet draped over a table or between chairs. Be sure to provide flashlights for those wild animals that they may encounter during the night!

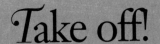

Take off!

Y ou and your grandchild can spend many hours at the airport just watching the take-offs and landings. Be sure to bring lunch or a snack and enjoy the show!

Extra, Extra!

*E*ncourage a future cub reporter with a tour of your local newspaper printing facility. It's great fun — you will enjoy it as much as your grandchild!

Build a house!

Grandpa, encourage that future homebuilder! Your local hardware stores have some great birdhouse kits you and your grandchild can build together. Be sure to find out what types of birds are in your neighborhood and purchase the proper housing.

Let's make a deal!

*B*ring out that deck of cards and spend some great times with your grandchild playing cribbage or hearts. Today might be the day to teach your grandchild some ageless card games!

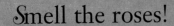

*C*heck out your local botanical gardens. You might find some classes to share with your grandchild such as flower arranging or gardening. Nature and grandchildren go so well together!

Take a walk!

Get away from interruptions and distractions. Hold hands, watch clouds, walk in puddles — make some memories!

Board?

Grandpa, on a rainy day, teach your grandchild a wonderful board game like chess or checkers. Remember to have lots of patience and occasionally let them win!

Picture this!

*H*ave your grandchild bring over a family album to share with you. Then dust off one of your old picture albums to share with them. Take turns sharing a page at a time.

Catch a ride!

*T*ake a simple trip with your grandchild. A local bus, train or ferry will ensure a fun adventure!

If the piece fits!

*N*othing is quite as inviting as a jigsaw puzzle set up on a table. Leave it there as you and your grandchild progress with it. A great place to have some heart-felt conversations and smiles!

$\mathcal{L}$ick it!

$\mathcal{D}$on't forget your local post office for getting your grandchild started on their very first stamp collection! You just might be introducing a life-long hobby!

Monopoly anyone?

*T*imeless board games such as Monopoly and Scrabble can provide hours of fun. Perhaps you could ask your grandchild to bring their favorite board game with them! They now have Monopoly Junior and Scrabble Junior for younger ages too.

Lights — Camera — Action!

$\mathcal{V}$isit your local TV station or radio station. This can be especially fun if you are able to be in an audience for a live show!

*F*lower pot art!

*P*urchase some inexpensive clay pots. Get the appropriate paints from your local hobby store and the let your grandchild use their imagination. Your young artist will love it!

Green thumb?

*N*ow that you have your one-of-a-kind flower pot — fill it! Shop with your grandchild for some flower seeds. Fill the bottom of the pot with pebbles and plant according to the directions. Then have fun watching them grow!

King/Queen for the day!

Sick grandchild? Make them feel like royalty with lots of pillows, stuffed animals, books, magazines, etc. Offer drinks in iced mugs with bows, colorful straws or floating fruit. Parfaits on an elegant tray covered with comics or pretty magazine pictures will be sure to get a smile!

Create a chef!

*A*sk your grandchild for their choice of a favorite meal. Then go shopping for the ingredients and prepare the meal together.

A penny for your thoughts!

A nother wonderful life-long hobby can be coin collecting. Your local hobby store will have the materials needed to start this project.

*F*ore!

*K*ids and miniature golf just naturally go together. Challenge your grandchild to eighteen holes. Good for almost all ages — and lots of fun!

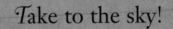

Take to the sky!

*T*ake advantage of those windy days. Get a colorful kite and head for the park or local baseball field. Take a blanket to sit on and perhaps a thermos of cocoa to share!

Play it up!

$\mathcal{S}$hare the experience of the theater with your grandchild. Check your local college, high schools or theater for age-appropriate productions.

Share yourself!

*D*o you have a special hobby? It might be gathering and pressing flowers, knitting, bird watching, carpentry or whittling! Teach your grandchild!

Lost your marbles?

*P*urchase some marbles from a hobby store. It's a great game to play with your grandchild on a rainy day. One great marble game is Box Marbles. Turn a shoe box on its side and score points by getting a marble to stop inside the box. It's great fun!

Looking upward!

*D*oes your city have an observatory? Find out what the hours of operation are and go! This is especially fun if you and/or your grandchild have some knowledge of the constellations. Read up on the stars before you go!

Author, author!

Create some new stories at bedtime. Ask your grandchild to complete the story you begin with "Penelope, the pink giraffe, was eating purple leaves when all of a sudden ...". Stimulate further adventures with "And then, Heathcliff, her long time friend said 'Penelope, you have green dots all over you! Why?'". You might want to record your stories on an audio cassette.

Tee up!

*C*reate your own miniature golf course in your back yard! Bury small yogurt containers to use as the golf holes. Then use bricks, boards, toy car tracks, rocks, hardware, etc. to make the course. For young children tennis balls might be easier to use than golf balls.

Booster Club!

*I*f you live close to your grandchildren, attend some of their athletic events. Surprise them and show up for practice. You might even consider assisting the coach. So . . . volunteer!

Bird wash!

Create an oasis for the birds with your grandchild. A large flower pot underliner makes an ideal birdbath. Place it on a tree stump (out of reach of neighborhood cats!) and arrange a few flat rocks on the bottom. Fill with less than three inches of water and watch the birds enjoy their new bath!

Make a friend!

*I*s there a child in your neighborhood close to the age of your grandchild? Contact them and have them meet each other. It could be the beginning of a very special friendship!

Projects, projects!

Your grandchild will enjoy participating with you in some of your fix-up projects. Repainting an old shed or fence will create lots of special conversation time. If the child is very young, use a bucket of water with a brush.

Special occasion?

Sit down with your grandchild and make something together for that very special occasion and then put it away for a surprise. Make a flag to fly on the 4th of July. Make a barn for your Christmas manger scene.

Shop 'til you drop!

Kids love the mall! Your grandchild will enjoy an afternoon shopping for some special occasion. Mom's birthday, sister's birthday, etc. can be great reasons for this fun outing!

Court is in session!

*Y*our local courthouse can be an interesting tour for you and your grandchild. Check with the bailiff to see that the case is age-appropriate for your grandchild.

What if?

While in the car together, you can play the "What If?" game. Stimulate conversation with questions such as "What if you were approached by a stranger?" or "What would you do if you could do anything you wanted?". Be creative. You can teach and learn many valuable things with these scenarios.

On the road again!

*A*nother good car game, especially for older children, is to select a long word, such as grandchildren, and see how many words they can make from it. Also, see how many different state license plates they can count before returning home. These are fun ways to pass time on the trip!

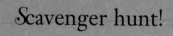

Scavenger hunt!

A great rainy day activity is to go to the mall and have a scavenger hunt. Use "items" such as finding a woman with twins, a man eating ice cream, a child crawling on the floor, or a pregnant woman. Good hunting!

A fun outdoor activity is to create a Frisbee course in your backyard. Strategically place barrels or trash cans around the yard to create the course and make up a point system for the Frisbee that lands in the container, close to it, etc.

Give your grandchildren the world!

*M*ost libraries allow you to check out eight or more books at one time. Videos and cassettes are also available. Imagine the wealth of information at your fingertips! Perhaps your grandchildren could read to you.

Plan an evening at the movies!

*W*ith parents suggestions, select a couple of videos that you and your grandchild can watch together. Make some popcorn, dim the lights and enjoy!

Constructive planning.

A trip to the local hobby store can stimulate a wealth of creative ideas for activities with your grandchild. Perhaps a model airplane, paint by number kit or jewelry making kit. The store clerk can help you make age-appropriate selections.

Conversation ticklers.

$\mathcal{K}$now your grandchild better by utilizing these conversation starters: "Tell me something good that has happened since the last time I saw you", or, "On a scale of 1 to 10, how is school this year - and why?", or "What is something you have done recently that you are proud of?", etc.

Big splash!

*A*ll children love to wash cars! Let your grandchild wash yours. Even a young child can clean windows, dry or wash wheels. You both benefit from this fun activity — especially on a hot, sunny day! Plan on getting wet!

*H*ome grown!

*M*any garden shops are eager to assist you and your grandchild in starting a garden. Plan what you will grow, get the necessary materials, select a corner of your yard and get digging!

Bicycle Rodeo.

Set up an obstacle course in your back yard or driveway for those bicycle-riding grandchildren! Make the course challenging. Then time them to see who can go through the fastest, slowest, etc. If your grandchildren are from out of town without their bikes, hit some yard sales or second-hand shops for a bargain bike.

What's happening?

*M*ost towns have a wealth of special events. Be watchful for those that would be fun for you and your grandchild. Events such as Sesame Street Live, Agape Kids, Disney on Ice or the circus are always popular.

Sports enthusiast.

*I*s your grandchild interested in a particular sport? Or all sports? Take grandchildren to a special sporting event of their choice one at a time. This is great one-on-one time!

*M*any wonderful movies are available for an afternoon in the theater. Most theaters have twilight, or matinee, prices. Check that the movie is age-appropriate. Perhaps you should also clear the movie with Mom or Dad. Have fun!

Class reunion!

$\mathcal{D}$ust off your old yearbook and show your grandchild what it was like at your school! Be prepared to laugh about those "weird" clothes and hairstyles! Look at your grandchild's yearbook. They will love to show you friends, teachers, etc.

*H*ow about a zoo-logical trip!

*P*ack a special lunch and take a trip to the local zoo. Call to find out if anything special is going on for the day you plan to go, such as feeding times. Remember that the animals are more active on cooler days!

Politics?

Yes, you and your grandchild can enjoy visiting the state legislature when it is in session. Go and see our government in action! You can find out the agenda prior to going to see if the bills might be of interest to your grandchild.

Old flicks!

*T*urn on that VCR and tape some wonderful old movies you've spotted in the TV guide. Perhaps a Busby-Birkley musical or an Andy Hardy movie. Add some popcorn and a few sodas and go to the movies!

*F*ire 101.

*F*or older grandchildren a skill that will always be needed is how to build a fire. Take the time to teach safety precautions and proper procedures, using your fireplace or a designated place out of doors. Then roast some marshmallows!

Operation — Information.

*D*oes your grandchild have a report coming up? Have them choose a city they would like to visit and write or call that city's Chamber of Commerce for information. The pictures and brochures of the area will make the report more interesting for them!

Voting with your grandchildren is the perfect time to explain polling procedures and the special privilege each of us has as a citizen of the United States!

Treasure Hunt!

$\mathcal{B}$efore your grandchild arrives hide household items such as pots, pans, spoons, bowls, etc. around the yard. Prizes for items found might be cookies or a piece of cake.

PRAISE your grandchild!

*N*oted psychologist, Dr. James Dobson, has said that it takes four praises for every criticism to keep up a child's self-esteem. Encourage your grandchild even in the small things and watch them glow!

Pound it, pull it, twist it!

Grandpa, your grandchild will have many hours of entertainment learning how to drive a nail into a block of wood and then using the other end of the hammer to pull it out. Teach them how to drive screws also; a great feeling of accomplishment!

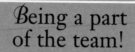

Being a part of the team!

*L*et your grandchild help with the chores! This simple idea can teach them to fold clothes, empty the dishwasher or shine shoes. The fun is doing it together!

Seeds of life.

$\mathcal{T}$ ake time during each visit to read together and learn of all of God's promises for our lives! Invest in a children's devotional book from your local Christian bookstore and you've made an invaluable investment in their lives!

I spy!

A t mealtime ask your grandchild what good deed they did, or saw someone do, for that day. Noting acts of forgiveness, compliments and helping others are wonderful life lessons!

Banker.

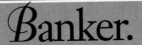

$\mathcal{Y}$our grandchild will love handling the money for an outing! This is a great opportunity to teach math and money skills by letting them pay the bills, tip or make change.

Sew it up!

S howing your grandchild how to sew the hem of a skirt or sew on a button will really make them feel a great sense of accomplishment.

*G*randpa, can you play the harmonica, whittle, whistle or tie knots? Try these together! These activities can spark some wonderful times of laughter and conversation.

Instant artist!

With bright crayons color a design all over a piece of paper. Then cover the design with black crayon. Have your grandchild use the edge of a paper clip to scratch off the black and the color design will show through!

Go sailing!

*M*ake paper boats out of newspaper and sail the seas in a local pond. You can color your sailboats, put designs on them and have races! Bottle cap boats and walnut boats are fun, too!

Crafty idea!

*T*ry a new craft for both of you. Quilting and smocking are fun. How about making a decorator pillow? A fabric store can help get you started.

Button, button, who has the button?

$\mathcal{D}$o you have a button box? Have your grandchild sort them by size and color. Perhaps they could string them into a necklace or belt!

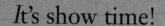

*R*emember how fun it was to act out a play for your parents? Plan one for your grandchildren! Hit the closet for costumes and maybe you'll encourage a future thespian!

Driving game!

$\mathcal{F}$ind a local classical station on the car radio and see who can pick out the different instruments being used. For older children see if they can guess the composer before the announcer tells you!

Pumpkin decorating contest!

Markers and sparkles for little ones and a carving knife for older children can create some masterpieces under your supervision. Great way to celebrate Fall!

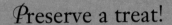

Preserve a treat!

*F*ind a local "You Pick 'Em" berry patch and try your hand at canning! Simple directions are available in most cookbooks. If you aren't sure about canning, put up your berries in freezer bags.

Celebrate the 4th of July!

*L*et your grandchild pick out a favorite patriotic song and teach them all the verses. Go to the library and find out who wrote it and why. Some of our founding fathers can give us new meaning to some wonderful songs!

Old McDonald had a farm!

*D*o you know someone who lives on a farm? Visit in the Spring and see how baby animals are fed or how crops and gardens are planted.

Name that tune!

*A*nywhere, anytime, you can play this fun game. Hum a few bars of a familiar song and let your grandchild guess the tune.

Creative writing.

*H*elp your grandchild write and entire letter to a friend by cutting out words from an old magazine or newspaper. Tape them onto a piece on paper. Fun to do and fun to receive!

Redecorate!

*L*et your grandchild help you rearrange furniture, move pictures, etc. for a new look!

*A*cquisition!

*C*ollections are always popular. Collect different leaves together. Iron them between wax paper and label. Your library has books to help you identify the different types. This makes a great project for "Show and Tell" at school.

Get crafty!

*A*ttend a craft fair with your grandchild. Get some great ideas and try to copy them together at home!

Save a life!

With older children take a C.P.R. class. Local hospitals and Red Cross Centers will have classes available. This could be an invaluable life-saving tool!

Milk-shake extravaganza!

$\mathcal{U}$se some imagination in your creations. Try honey, berries, bananas, flavoring, etc. Then surprise someone with a treat!

Name it!

Grandchildren, go through the photo albums with your grandparents. Label names of the people. Put funny descriptions under some of the photos. Many years from now they will thank you for your thoughtfulness!

Create an arborist!

𝓟lant a tree together and watch it grow right alongside your grandchild!

Go fish!

*I*t's never too late to learn to fish. Go to your local sporting goods store for lessons. Grab a line and go fishin'! Don't forget to check into getting a fishing license!

YMCA!

*E*scape to your local YMCA for hours of fun for your grandchild. Most have programs available all summer and indoor swimming for fun in the winter.

Reach out!

*D*o you have your grandchild the same day every week? Try volunteering an hour of each week at a local nursing home. Read to the residents, pass out candy or just stop and visit.

Create a castle!

*O*r a doghouse, or playhouse! This rainy day activity is easy with a big box, paints or markers. Your grandchild's imagination will do the rest!

Look at the birdie!

*A*nother life-long hobby can be created with a bird book from your local Audubon Society. Spend some time trying to find some birds described in the book and learn about them.

*W*hat is the good news and bad news about soccer (or whatever sport they play) this year? What do you like about Girl Scouts? Boy Scouts? Dancing? The topics are as limitless as your imagination!

Smith for Senate!

*F*or the older grandchild, get them interested in a local or statewide political campaign. This can teach wonderful lessons about issues, candidates and how a position is won. They will also become much more aware of our local politics!

Word scrabble.

*F*or "waiting" times such as at the doctor or dentist, print a large word, such as Thanksgiving, and each of you see how many words you can make from it. Time it. Then share a special "treat" as your prizes!

Neighborhood treasure hunt!

$\mathcal{L}$ ike you did in your house, send your grandchild to "find" special items at your neighbors. Make it easy for your neighbors — items such as rubber bands, newspapers, pencils, bottle caps, etc.

Read the Bible together!

*F*ind a translation appropriate for your grandchild's age. Your local Christian book store can help you make the best selection.

Walk in the rain!

*S*plash in the puddles! Rainy days aren't just meant for indoors. Your grandchild and you can share much laughter as you make a memory of your rainy day walk!

Summer camp!

*T*here are wonderful camps that specialize in grandparents bringing their grandchildren. Activities include picking raspberries, singing around a campfire, sharing meals and many others. They even have activities scheduled to give grandma and grandpa a rest time, or a chance to attend seminars.

Summer camp locations!

*T*here are two camp locations. One is in a former Vanderbilt retreat in New York's Adirondacks. Both camps are sponsored by the Foundation for Grandparenting, a non-profit organization designed to foster the bond between grandparents and kids. For information send a self-addressed envelope to the Foundation for Grandparenting, Box 326, Cohasset, MA. 02025.

About the Author

Margolyn Woods is a popular speaker on the Christian speakers' circuit. She is a former Rose Bowl Queen and actress.

Margolyn lives on a farm in Oklahoma with her husband Roy and three of their five children. She is the proud grandma of Megan Stewart!

Additional copies of this book are
available at your local bookstore.

P.O. Box 55388
Tulsa, Oklahoma 74155